ضرب المثل های دری افغانستان

Seanfhocail na hAfganastáine le Pictiúir
i nGaeilge, i nDaraí agus i mBéarla

ضرب المثل های دری افغانستان

Seanfhocail na hAfganastáine le Pictiúir

Collected and originally
translated into English by
Edward Zellem

ادوارد زالم

Translated into Irish by Gordon McCoy
with Irish Equivalents by
Fionnuala Carson Williams

Cultures Direct Press

For the children of

Afghanistan and Ireland

Dedication

This book is respectfully dedicated

to the people of Afghanistan,

and to those who are working together with them

to bring lasting peace and security.

اهداء

این کتاب، با کمال احترام، به مردم افغانستان و آنهایی که همراه با آنان
برای تأمین صلح و امنیت پایدار تلاش می‌کنند، اهدا می‌گردد.

As the Proverb says:

چنانچه این ضرب‌المثل می‌گوید:

کوه هر قدر بلند باشد،

سر خود راه دارد.

Koh har qadar beland baashad,

sar-e khod raah daarad.

Even if a mountain is very high,

it has a path to the top.

Dari Language Facts

نکته هایی درباره ی زبان دری

- Dari is one of the two official languages of Afghanistan. The other is Pashto.

- Dari is the common language used in most business and government in Afghanistan.

- Dari is a very ancient and respected language. Some have called it the language of kings.

- Many people think Dari is an older form of Persian Farsi, the main language of Iran. The two languages have many similarities.

- There are 32 letters in the Dari alphabet. Twenty-eight of them are the same as the Arabic alphabet. The extra four letters are used for sounds that are not in the Arabic language.

- Dari is written right to left. There is no upper or lower case. The shapes of Dari letters can change, depending on where they are in a word.

About Afghanistan

درباره ی افغانستان

Afghanistan is a beautiful and interesting country. It is an ancient land between South and Central Asia.

It is famous for its high mountains and cold winters, but some places in Afghanistan are very flat and dry.

Afghanistan is slightly larger than France in land area. It has 30 million people and many different ethnic groups and tribes. The largest ethnic groups are Pashtuns, Tajiks, Hazaras and Uzbeks. Almost all Afghans are Muslims.

AFGHANISTAN

Administrative Divisions

UZBEKISTAN
★ DUSHANBE
TAJIKISTAN
CHINA

TURKMENISTAN

Faizābād

JOWZJĀN
Shibirghān

Mazār-e
Sharif

KUNDUZ

Kunduz

Tāloqān

BADAKHSHĀN

TAKHĀR

BALKH

Aibak

Pārūn

FĀRYĀB

Sar-e
Pul

SAMANGĀN

BAGHLĀN

NŪRISTĀN

Maimanah

Pul-e
Khumrī

PANJSHIR

BĀDGHĪS

SAR-E PUL

Bāzārak

Chārikar

Mahmūd-e
Rāqi

Asadābād

Qal'ah-ye Now

Bāmyān

PARWĀN

KUNAR

Herāt

Chaghcharān

BĀMYĀN

KĀPISA

Mehtar Lām

ISLAMABAD
★

INDIA

HERĀT

GHŌR

WARDAK

KABUL

LAGHMĀN

★ KĀBUL

Maidān
Shahr

Jalālābād

Maidān
Shahr

LŌGAR

NANGARHĀR

Nīlī

Pul-e 'Alam

PAKTIYĀ

DĀYKUNDĪ

Ghaznī

Gardēz

Farāh

GHAZNĪ

KHŌST

Khōst

FARĀH

Tārin
Kot

Sharan

URUZGĀN

ZĀBUL

PAKTĪKĀ

PAKISTAN

IRAN

Lashkar
Gāh

Kandahār

Qalāt

Zaranj

HELMAND

KANDAHĀR

NĪMRŌZ

1972 Line of Control

	International boundary
	Province *(welāyat)* boundary
★	National capital
⊙	Province *(welāyat)* capital

Afghanistan has 34 provinces (welāyat).

0   50   100   150 Kilometers
0   50   100   150 Miles

Scale 1:6,900,000

*Dilaram District is reported to be administered from Farah Province,
but the Government of Afghanistan does not recognize its existence.

Boundary representation is
not necessarily authoritative.

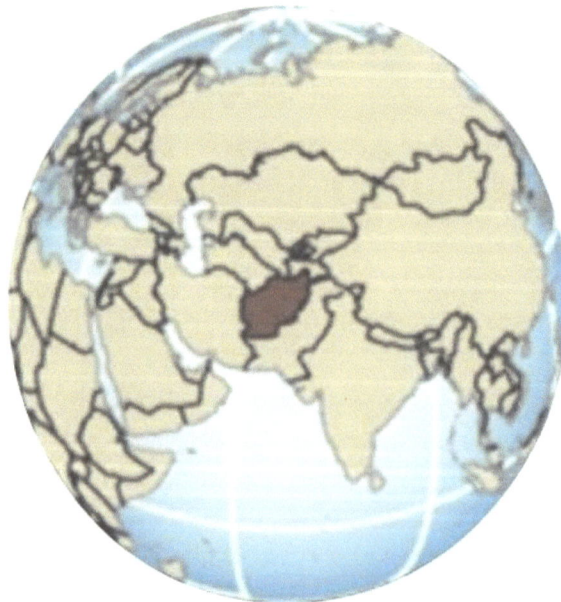

Phonetic Pronunciation Guide

رهنمای تلفظ

- "kh" is a "k" sound combined with "h" sound, made in the back of the throat as if clearing it.

- "oy" rhymes with "boy."

- "e" when attached to the end of a word sounds like "ay," as in "hay."

- "r" is a roll of the "r" sound across the tongue.

- "ey/ay" rhymes with "hay."

- "mey" sounds like "may" with a soft "y" sound.

- "gh" is a "g" sound combined with an "h" sound, made in the back of the throat as if clearing it.

The Dari Alphabet

الفبا دری

ث	ت	پ	ب	ا
sey (s)	tey (t)	pey (p)	bey (b)	alef (a)

د	خ	ح	چ	ج
daal (d)	khey (kh)	hey (h)	chey (ch)	jeem (j)

س	ژ	ز	ر	ذ
seen (s)	zhey (zh)	zey (z)	rey (r)	zaal (z)

ظ	ط	ض	ص	ش
zoy (z)	toy (t)	zuwat (z)	suwat (s)	sheen (sh)

ک	ق	ف	غ	ع
kaaf (k)	qaaf (q)	fey (f)	ghayn (gh)	eyn (e)

و	ن	م	ل	گ
wow (w)	noon (n)	meem (m)	laam (l)	gaaf (g)

ی	ه
yaa (y)	hey (h or aa)

The Irish Proverbs

Every Dari proverb is followed by its **literal translation** in both English and Irish. Each Irish-language **proverb** is placed below the **meaning** of the Dari proverb and is followed by its literal translation in English in square brackets, and its source. The Irish proverbs were all collected in the twentieth century by school children and their teachers in a plan by the Irish Folklore Department in conjunction with the Department of Education. It was called 'The Schools' Collection Scheme'. Through it the older girls and boys, up to the school leaving age of 14, in the National Schools sought proverbs (and other folklore) from their families and neighbors. This resulted in a huge collection of proverbs in both Irish and English. It forms part of the National Folklore Collection, University College Dublin (NFC) and can be accessed online at https://**www.duchas.ie**/en/cbes. Today Irish is spoken as a community language in only some of the 32 land divisions or counties of Ireland. In order to aid their comprehension, the Schools' Collection Scheme proverbs have been rendered in a modern orthography which does not alter the original pronunciation, for example, *teintean* > *tinteán* and relative pronouns have been introduced where they were absent. Dialectal forms have, however, been preserved, for example, *tarann* (Standard Irish *tagann* 'comes') and *asacáin* (Standard Irish *achasán* 'reproach').

I wish to thank the Director of the National Folklore Collection, University College Dublin, for permission to publish the proverbs from it here, Gordon McCoy who made literal translations in Irish of the literal English translations that were provided for all the Dari proverbs, and Ruairí Ó Bléine who kindly checked the draft and translated the cover.

- FCW

فرصت

Forsat

Opportunity

ماهی را هر وقت

از آب بگیری،

تازه است.

Maahee-raa har waqt az aab biggeree, taaza ast.

**When you take a fish
from the water, it is always fresh.**

Nuair a thógann tú iasc as an uisce,
bíonn sé i gcónaí úr.

Meaning of the Proverb:
It is never too late to begin something new.
When you begin something, it always is a fresh start.

**Tá iasc san bhfarraige chomh maith
is a gabhadh riamh.**
[There are as good fish in the sea as were ever caught.]

NFC School Manuscript 0140, page 124, County Mayo.

قدر دانی

Qadr-danee

Gratitude

كفش كهنه در بيابان نعمت است.

Kafsh-e kohna dar beyaabaan neamat ast.

Old sandals in the desert are a blessing.

Is beannaithe iad seanchuaráin san ghaineamhlach.

Meaning of the Proverb:
Even if something is old or plain, it is valuable if it works and meets your needs. Be grateful for what you have, and you will receive what you really need.

Is fearr leathbhuilín ná bheith gan arán.
[Half a loaf is better than to be without bread.]

NFC School Manuscript 0130, page 245 County Mayo.

موفق

Mowafaq

Successful

كوه هر قدر بلند باشد،

سر خود راه دارد.

Koh har qadar beland baashad,
sar-e khod raah daarad.

Even if a mountain is very high,
it has a path to the top.

Cé gur fíor-ard an sliabh,
bíonn cosán go barr aige.

Meaning of the Proverb:
Nothing is impossible. There is always a way.

As a chéile a níthear na caisleáin.
[Castles are made one at a time.]

NFC School Manuscript 1072, page 090, County Donegal.

تحصیل

Tahseel

Education

ز گهواره تا گور دانش بجوی.

Ze gahwaara taa guhr, daanesh bejoye.

Seek knowledge from cradle to grave.

Bí ag lorg eolais ón chliabhán
go dtí an uaigh.

Meaning of the Proverb:
Never stop learning, whether
you are young or old.

قوى

Qa-wee

Strong

صد زدن زرگر،
یک زدن آهنگر.

Sad zadan-e zar-gar,
yak zadan-e aahan-gar.

A hundred strikes by a goldsmith,
one strike by a blacksmith.

Céad buille ag an ghabha óir,
buille amháin ag an ghabha dhubh.

Meaning of the Proverb:
It is better to act once with strength
and finish something, instead of
acting weakly many times.

Is fearr cleas amháin maith ná lán
mála de chleasanna gan mhaith.
[One good trick is better than a bagful of bad tricks.]

NFC School Manuscript 1069, page 006, County Donegal.

برابری

Baraa-baree

Equality

همه را به یک چشم نگاه کنید.

Hama-raa ba yak chashm negaah kuneed.

Everyone should be looked at with the same eye.

Is leis an tsúil amháin is ceart
gach duine a bhreathnú.

Meaning of the Proverb:
Treat everyone as an equal. Do not discriminate against people because of their religion, race, gender, skin color or nationality.

Ná déan feoil as iasc daofa.

[Don't make of them meat out of fish]

NFC School Manuscript 1064, page 031, County Donegal.

شخصيت

Shakh-seeyat

Character

نمد سیاه به شستن
سفید نمی‌شود.

*Namad-e see-ya ba shustan
safed na-mey-shawad.*

Black carpet cannot become white by washing.

Ní dhéanfaidh an níochán brat
urláir bán den bhrat urláir dubh.

Meaning of the Proverb:
If a person is bad by nature, he cannot easily
become good. It can be hard to lead a bad
person to the right path.

**Nífidh uisce gach uile
cineál ach an peacadh.**
[Water will wash every kind of thing but sin.]
NFC School Manuscript 1064, page 033, County Donegal.

**An rud atá sa smior is doiligh
a bhaint as an chnáimh.**
[What's in the marrow
is difficult to take out of the bone.]
NFC School Manuscript 1064, page 001, County Donegal.

آفریننده

Aa-fareen-enda

Creativity

ضرورت مادر ایجاد است.

Zaroorat maadar-e ejaad ast.

Need is the mother of invention.

Is é an gá máthair na cumadóireachta.

Meaning of the Proverb:
People are usually creative and
resourceful if they need something.

Múineann gá seift.
[Necessity teaches invention.]

NFC School Manuscript 0318, page 263, County Cork.

(English proverb is the same as the Dari:
"Necessity is the mother of invention.")

تحمل

Tah-mal

Tolerance

عیسی به دین خود،

موسی به دین خود.

Isa ba deen-e khod, Mousa ba deen-e khod.

Jesus to his religion, and Moses to his.

Bíodh a chreideamh féin ag Íosa,
agus a chreideamh féin ag Maois.

Meaning of the Proverb:
All people have the right to choose what they do,
think or feel. Everyone should respect and be
tolerant of the religions, beliefs and opinions of others.

Gach duine lena dhuine fhéin.
[Everyone with his own people.]
NFC School Manuscript 1064, page 016, County Donegal.

**Gach éan mar a oiltear é agus
an fhuiseog sa mhónaidh.**
[Every bird as it is reared and the skylark
(*Alauda arvensis*) for the bog.]
NFC School Manuscript 1064, page 016, County Donegal.

تزوير

Tazweer

Trickery

بار کج به منزل نمی‌رسد.

Baar-e kaj ba manzel na-mey-rasad.

A tilted load doesn't reach its destination.

Ní féidir leat ceann scríbe a bhaint
amach agus d'ualach ag dul ar fiar.

Meaning of the Proverb:
Bad always loses, and good always wins in the end.

Note: The illustration for this Proverb refers to a Dari fable about a fox who liked
to play tricks. The fox tricked the goose by giving him soup on a plate. The goose
could not eat it because of its long beak. The next day, the goose gave soup to the fox
in a jar with a long neck. The fox could not eat it because his short nose
would not fit into the jar. So the goose had the last laugh.

Más gasta an madadh rua gabhtar é sa deireadh.

[Although the fox is fast it is caught in the end.]

NFC School Manuscript 1064, page 025, County Donegal.

Is mairg nach siúlann go díreach.

[Woe to the one who doesn't walk straight.]

NFC School Manuscript 1064, page 023, County Donegal.

ابله

Abla

Silly

با هر چیز بازی،
با ریش بابا هم بازی.

Baa har-cheez baazi,
baa reesh-e baa-baa ham baazi.

Joking about everything,
even Grandfather's beard.

Gach rud ina cheap magaidh,
féasóg an tseanathar, fiú.

Meaning of the Proverb:
Someone who takes nothing seriously and makes
jokes about everything can get into trouble. Often
said to a person who is "crossing the line."

An té a bíos gan chéill bíonn sé ag magadh.
[The senseless person mocks.]

NFC School Manuscript 1066, page 024, County Donegal.

(English expression: "Playing with fire.")

وفاداری

Wafaa-daary

Loyalty

تو به مه، مه به تو.

Tu ba ma, ma ba tu.

You to me, me to you.

Déan domh agus déanfar duit.

Meaning of the Proverb:
If you do good things for me, I will do them for you.
We will take care of each other.

An té atá go maith dhuit bí go maith dhó.
[Be good to the person who is good to you.]

NFC School Manuscript 0130, page 257 County Mayo.

(English proverb: "You scratch my back,
and I'll scratch yours.")

اغراق

Egh-raaq

Exaggeration

از کاه ، کوه نساز.

Az kaah, koh nasaaz.

Don't make a mountain from straw.

Ná déan sliabh as cochán.

Meaning of the Proverb:
Don't make something into more than it is.
Don't exaggerate.

(English proverb: "Don't make
a mountain out of a molehill.")

امکانات

Emkaanaat

Possibilities

سر زنده باشه،

کلاه بسیار است.

Sar zenda baasha, kolaah besyaar ast.

**If there is life in your head,
there are lots of hats.**

Más beo do cheann,
is iomaí hata a chaithfear.

Meaning of the Proverb:
Being alive means it is possible to become
anything, if you work hard and have faith.

ريا

Reyaa

Hypocrisy

روز ملنگ ، شو پلنگ.

Roz malang, shao palang.

Daytime a saint, night time a tiger.

Naomh sa lá, tíogar san oíche.

Meaning of the Proverb:
This describes someone who pretends to be a
good person but does bad things
when no one can see.

Béal eidhinn agus croí cuilinn.

[An ivy (*Hedera*) mouth and a holly (*Ilex*) heart.]

Note: That is, a soft or sweet-talking mouth but inside a prickly or hard heart.
An ivy leaf is soft but a holly leaf is prickly.

NFC School Manuscript 0096, page 177, County Mayo.

مسئوليت

Massoul-iat

Responsibility

برف بام خوده
به بام ما ننداز.

Barf-e baam-e khod-a
ba baam-e maa nandaaz.

Don't throw snow from your own roof to ours.

Ná caith an sneachta ó do dhíon
féin ar an díon s'againne.

Meaning of the Proverb:
Don't blame other people for your own mistakes,
or try to pass your troubles off onto them.

**Achasán an chorcáin leis an gciotal,
"Tá tú dubh!" arsa an corcán
leis an gciotal.**
[The pot's complaint about the kettle
"You're black," said the pot to the kettle.]

NFC School Manuscript 0461, page 118, County Kerry.

خانه

Khanna

Home

هر کس را وطنش کشمیر است.

Har kas-ra watan-ash Kashmir ast.

Everyone's homeland is Kashmir to them.

Is Caismír do chách
a cheantar dúchais féin.

Meaning of the Proverb:
Afghan people think that the land of Kashmir
is a beautiful place. All people have an attachment
to their home and where they came from.

Níl aon tinteán mar do thinteán féin.

[There's no fireside like your own fireside.]

NFC School Manuscript 0318, page 259, County Cork.

تلاش

Talash

Effort

تا جان بتن است،
جان بکن است.

Ta jaan batan ast, jaan bekan ast.

While we live, we strive.

A fhad agus a mhairimid,
bímid ag streachailt.

Meaning of the Proverb:
Life is full of challenges. People must
work hard to overcome them.

Is iomaí cor sa tsaol.
[There's many a twist to life.]

NFC School Manuscript 0931, page 381, County Monaghan.

تمرین

Tamreen

Practice

بنویس، بنویس،

تا شوی خوش‌نویس.

Benawees, benawees,
taa sha-wee khosh nawees.

**Write, write,
to become a good writer.**

Coinnigh ort ag scríobh le bheith
i do scríbhneoir maith.

Meaning of the Proverb:
If you work hard at something and practice,
you will become better at it.

As an obair a gheibhtear an fhoghlaim.

[It is through work that learning is obtained.]

NFC School Manuscript 0642, page 212, County Mayo.

(English proverb: "Practice makes perfect.")

كيفيت

Kayfeeyat

Quality

خر تیز بهتر از
اسپ آهسته است.

Khar-e teyz behtar az asp-e aahesta ast.

A fast donkey is better than a slow horse.

Is fearr asal gasta ná capall mall.

Meaning of the Proverb:

Choose what is really best, not what looks best.

**Is fearr marcaíocht ar ghabhar
ná coisíocht dá fheabhas.**

[Riding on a goat is better than the best walking.]

NFC School Manuscript 0104, page 020, County Mayo.

امید

Omeed

Hope

پشت هر تاریکی،

روشنی است.

Pusht-e har taareekee, roshanee ast.

After every darkness is light.

Leanann an gile gach dorchadas.

Meaning of the Proverb:
Bad times will always pass
and things will become better.

**Tarann an ghrian amach
i ndiaidh na fearthainne.**

[The sun comes out after the rain.]
NFC School Manuscript 1065, page 135, County Donegal.

Dá fhad é an lá tiocfaidh an tráthnóna.

[However long the day, evening will come.]
NFC School Manuscript 0104, page 020, County Mayo.

احترام

Ehteraam

Respect

بهشت زیر
پای مادران است.

Behesht zer-e paay-e maadaraan ast.

Heaven is under the feet of mothers.

Is faoi chosa na máithreacha
a bhíonn na flaithis.

Meaning of the Proverb:
Mothers have a very important role in the world
and Heaven will reward them. You should
always respect your mother.

Bíonn an chlúdaigh fuar
nuair a imíos an mháthair.
[The chimney corner is cold
when the mother has gone.]

NFC School Manuscript 1064, page 008, County Donegal.

حقيقت

Haq-ee-qat

Truth

آفتاب به دو انگشت
پنهان نمی‌شود.

*Aaftaab ba doo angusht
pen-han na-mey-shawad.*

The sun cannot be hidden by two fingers.

Ní fholaíonn dhá mhéar an ghrian.

Meaning of the Proverb:
You cannot hide from the truth, just as
it is impossible to hold up two
fingers and block the sun.

Imíonn an bréag ach fanann an fhírinne.
[The falsehood goes but the truth remains.]

NFC School Manuscript 0096, p. 182, County Mayo.

(English proverb: "The truth will come out.")

ندامت

Nedaamat

Regret

پشت آب رفته،
بیل نگیر.

Pushte aab-e rafta, bel nageer.

Don't take a shovel to bring the water back.

Ná tóg sluasaid leis an
uisce a thabhairt ar ais.

Meaning of the Proverb:
When something bad happens
don't keep worrying about it – move on.

**Níl maith a bheith ag caint ar
an bhainne nuair atá sé doirte.**
[It's no good talking about the milk after it has spilt.]

NFC School Manuscript 1065, page 134, County Donegal.

خطرناک

Khattar-naak

Danger

تیغ را به دست
دیوانه دادن.

Tegh-raa ba dast-e daywaanah daadan.

**To give a sharp knife
to the hand of a maniac.**

Scian ghéar a chur i lámh an gheilt.

Meaning of the Proverb:
It is dangerous to give a big responsibility
to someone who is not ready for it,
or who will misuse it.

نمونه

Namuna

Sample

مشت نمونه‌ی

خروار است.

Mosht namuna-ye kharwar ast.

**A handful (of wheat) is
an example of the harvest.**

Is léiriu ar an fhómhar crag chruithneachta.

Meaning of the Proverb:
A small sample can show the
character of the whole thing.

حد

Hud

Limit

پایت را به اندازه‌ی
گلیمت دراز کن.

*Paayat-ra ba andaaza-ye
gelemat daraaz kon.*

Extend your legs to the length of your carpet.

Sín do chosa fad do bhrat urláir.

Meaning of the Proverb:
Don't attempt more than you can handle.

Caithfidh tú do chóta a ghearradh de réir do ghréasáin.

[You have to cut your coat according
to your roll of cloth.]

NFC School Manuscript 1072, page 096, County Donegal.

تعجب

Tajob

Surprise

از آنکه نمی‌دا نی بدان.

Az aan-ke na-mey-danee bedaan.

Expect the unexpected.

Bí ar d'airdeall don rud
nach bhfuil súil leis.

Meaning of the Proverb:
Be prepared for anything, even
shocking or surprising things.

Is iomdha rud a tharlaíonns
nach mbíonn dúil leis.

[Many a thing happens that isn't expected.]

NFC School Manuscript 0931, page 253, County Monaghan.

(There is an English proverb which is the
same as the Dari: "Expect the unexpected.")

بی انصافانه

Bey-ensaa-fanaa

Unfair

نخوردیم از آشش،
کور شدیم از دودش.

Nakhordeym az aashesh,
kor shudeym az doodesh.

We didn't eat the soup,
but were blinded by the smoke.

Níor ól muid an t-anraith
ach dalladh ag an toit muid.

Meaning of the Proverb:
To do all the work but receive none of the benefits.
Also: To pay more for something than it is worth.

(**Note:** Afghan people often cook "aash," a type of
noodle soup, over an open fire.)

Obair a mhallaidh Dia obair
gan bhia gan pháighe.
[God renounces work unrewarded by food or pay.]

NFC School Manuscript 0934, page 349, County Monaghan.

همکاری

Ham-kaaree

Co-operation

به یک گَل، بهار نمی‌شه.

Ba yak gul, bahaar na-mey-sha.

One flower doesn't bring spring.

Ní thig an t-earrach leis an bhláth amháin.

Meaning of the Proverb:
One person's work is usually not enough to finish
a job – it takes teamwork. **Also:** You should not be
content just because one good thing happens.

Ní dhéanann fáinleog amháin an samhradh.

[One swallow doesn't make the summer.]

Note: The swallow (*Hirundinidae* family) is one of the
migratory birds which visits Ireland (and Afghanistan)
from the Southern Hemisphere in the summer.

NFC School Manuscript 1091, page 038, County Donegal.

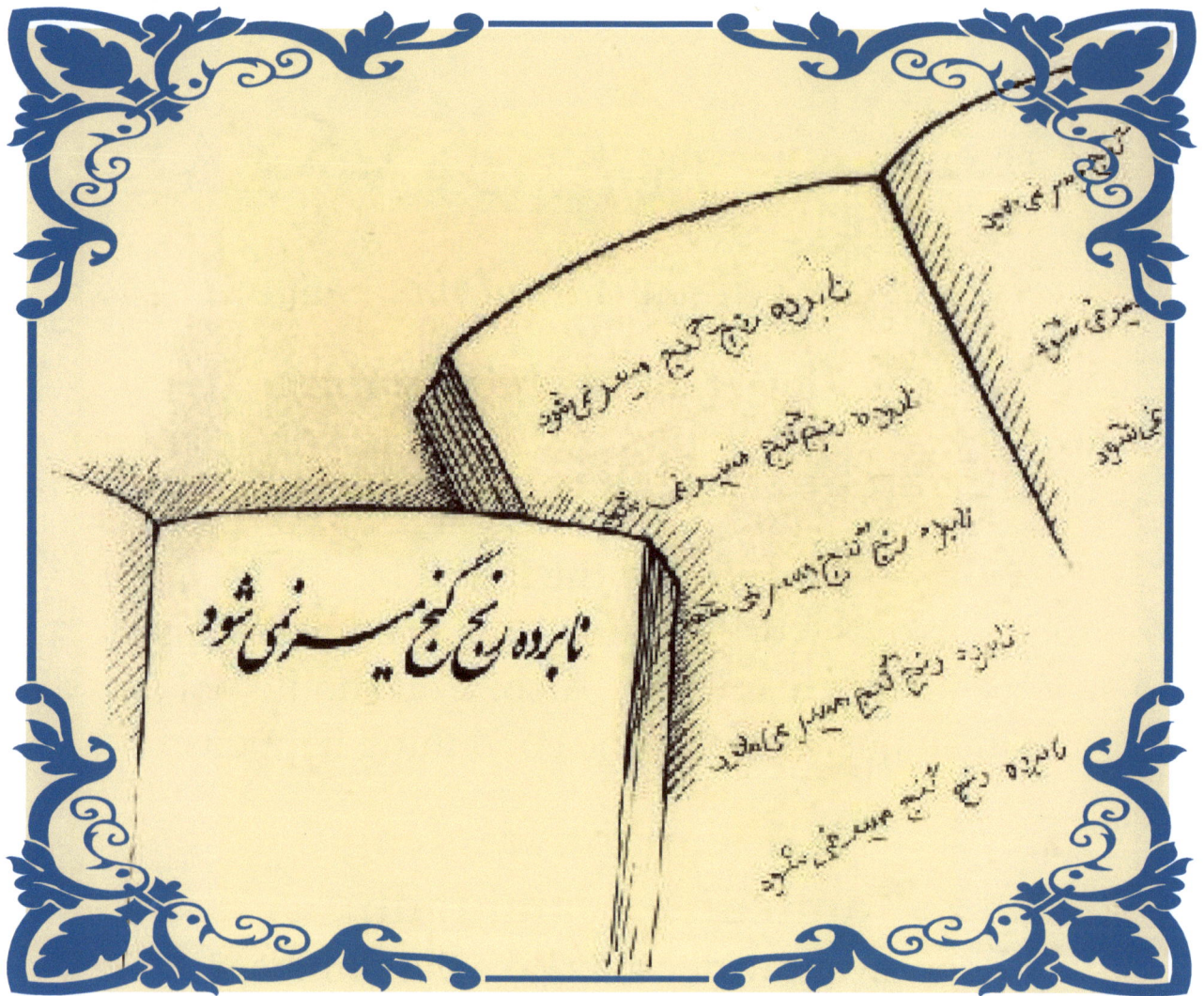

حوصله

Hawsela

Patience

دیر آید، درست آید.

Deyr aayad, dorost aayad.

Comes late, comes right.

An rud a dhéantar go mall, déantar i gceart é.

Meaning of the Proverb:
Better to work slowly and well than quickly and badly.

Tagann gach maith le cairde.

[Every good thing comes through time.]

NFC School Manuscript 0461, page 082, County Kerry.

Éist le tuile na habhna agus gabhfaidh tú breac.

[Listen to the noise of the river and you'll catch a trout.]

NFC School Manuscript 0931, page 254, County Monaghan.

Nuair is mó an deifir is mó an mhoill.

[When there's most hurry there's most delay.]

NFC School Manuscript 0083, page 127, County Galway.

Ní thagann luas is léireacht le céile.

[Speed and precision aren't compatible.]

NFC School Manuscript 0462, page 691, County Kerry.

An té a ritheas a thiteas.

[The one who runs falls.]

NFC School Manuscript 1072, page 089, County Donegal.

چانس بد

Chans-e-bad

Unlucky

آش را ناخورده، دهن سوخته.

Aash-ra naa-khorda, dahan sokhtah.

**Without eating any soup,
got a burned mouth.**

Dódh an béal agam gan anraith a ithe.

Meaning of the Proverb:
Someone who suffers or pays a heavy
price without gaining any benefit.

Obair a mhallaidh Dia obair
gan bhia gan pháighe.
[God renounces work unrewarded by food or pay.]

NFC School Manuscript 0934, page 349, County Monaghan.

زیبایی

Zebaa-ye

Beauty

گل پشت و روی ندارد.

Gul pusht wa rui na-daarad.

A flower has no front or back.

Níl cúl ná tosach ar an bhláth.

Meaning of the Proverb:
Used to praise the overall beauty,
delicacy or symmetry of something.

Also: A polite response when a person apologizes
for having his or her back turned toward you.

با عزم

Ba-ezm

Determination

قطره قطره دریا می‌شه.

Qattra qattra daryaa mey-sha.

A river is made drop by drop.

Braon ar bhraon a dhéantar an abhainn.

Meaning of the Proverb:
Even small efforts can produce big
results over time. Don't give up – good
things take time and patience.

Tiomsaíonn brobh beart
agus líontar sac le póiríní.
[Wisps assembled make a bundle
and small potatoes would fill a sack.]

NFC School Manuscript 0136, page 297, County Mayo.

Beagán go minic a líonann an sparán.
[Little and often fills the purse.]

NFC School Manuscript 1072, page 093, County Donegal.

ظرفیت

Zarfiat

Capability

دو تربوز به یک
دست گَرفته نمی‌شود.

Doo tarbuz ba yak dast gerefta na-mey-shawad.

**You can't hold two
watermelons in one hand.**

Ní féidir dhá mhealbhacán uisce
a iompar leis an lámh amháin.

Meaning of the Proverb:
Don't attempt more than you can handle,
or, something that is impossible.

Ní thig leis an ghobadán an
dá thráigh a fhreastal.

[The wading bird can't attend two strands.]
NFC School Manuscript 1073, page 441, County Donegal.

Chá dtig le duine bheith ag feadalaigh
agus ag ithe mine san am chéanna.

[It isn't possible for a person to whistle
and eat meal at the same time.]
NFC School Manuscript 1064, page 012, County Donegal.

غلطى

Ghalatee

Mistake

از خاطر یک کیک،
گلم را نسوزان.

Az khaater-e yak kaik,
gelem-raa na-suzaan.

Don't burn a carpet for a flea.

Ná dóigh brat urláir ar
mhaithe le dearnad.

Meaning of the Proverb:
Don't over-react to a problem, or make
a big mistake to cover up a small one.

هوشیار

Hoosh-yar

Cleverness

طفل خورد هوشیار
بهتر از کلان جاهل.

*Tefl-e khord-e hoosh-yar
behtar az kalaan-e jaahel.*

**A clever little child is
better than a foolish adult.**

Is fear leanbh beag cliste ná amadán fásta.

Meaning of the Proverb:
A person who is clever and intelligent is
worth more than a person who is only strong.

Is fearr stuaim ná neart.
[Wit is better than strength.]

NFC School Manuscript 1064, page 019, County Donegal.

(English proverb: "Brains over brawn.")

خوشبین

Khosh-been

Optimism

دنیا با امید زنده است.

Doon-ya baa omeed zenda ast.

The world is alive with hope.

Tá an domhan beo le dóchas.

Meaning of the Proverb:
Always have hope, because there always is hope.

**Coinnigh suas do chroí,
tá lá maith ag teacht.**
[Keep up your heart, a good day is coming.]

NFC School Manuscript 1064, page 013, County Donegal.

Also by Edward Zellem
Winner of twelve international book awards

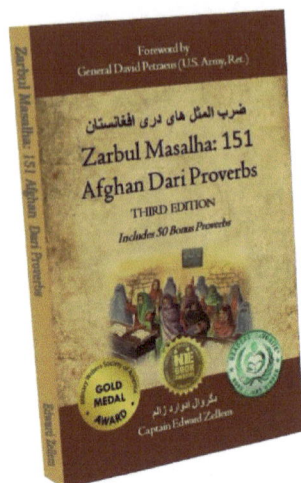

"Zarbul Masalha: 151 Afghan Dari Proverbs"

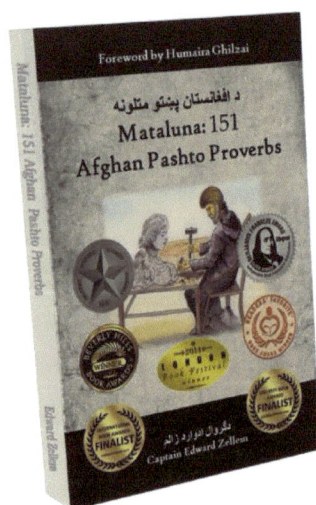

"Mataluna: 151 Afghan Pashto Proverbs"

Available now in over 115 countries

Learn more at www.afghansayings.com

Praise for *Zarbul Masalha, Mataluna* and *Afghan Proverbs Illustrated*

"Ed's Afghan Proverb books are a personal project, and some people say that they *help win hearts and minds*. I have always thought that 'winning hearts and minds' is an inaccurate way to say it, because 'winning' implies that somebody also *loses*. Nobody loses here. I think Ed's Afghan Proverbs books *connect* hearts and minds, which is a truly critical task."

- General David H. Petraeus (U.S. Army, ret)
Former commander of U.S.and ISAF forces in Afghanistan

"These proverbs are a reminder of old traditions and folklore that have been passed from generation to generation. And they are a true delight for anyone who has been away or alienated from Afghanistan."
- Leena Alam
Award-winning Afghan film actress and UNAMA Peace Ambassador

"Captain Zellem's collection is an outstanding work that underscores our common humanity."
- Dwight Jon Zimmerman
New York Times #1 best-selling author

"I call on all young Afghans to get a copy of this book. Your mothers will be dazzled to hear you speak using Proverbs. I have my book marked up with favorite Proverbs and every time I talk to Jeja, my mom, I throw out a new saying. It delights her to hear how much my Dari has improved."
- Humaira Ghilzai
World's top blogger on Afghan food and culture
www.afghancooking.net

"Captain Edward Zellem has written one of the most remarkable books in recent memory about Afghanistan."
- Veterans Radio Network

More Translations of *Afghan Proverbs Illustrated*

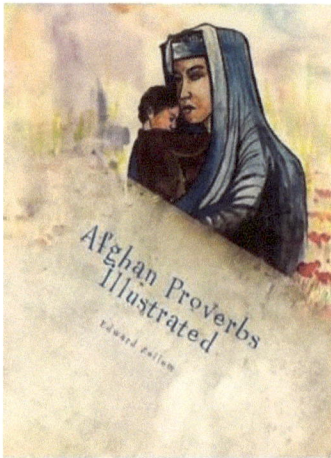
English

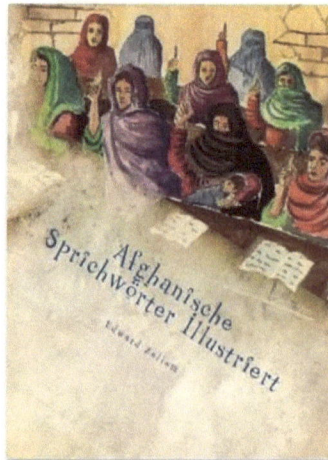
German

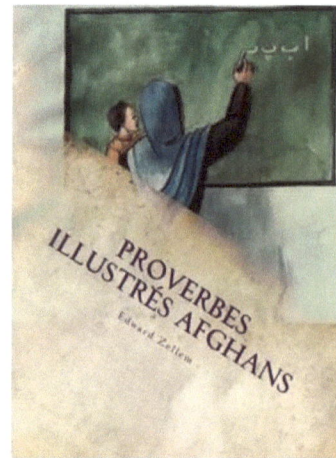
French

Russian

Polish

Portuguese

Swedish

Spanish

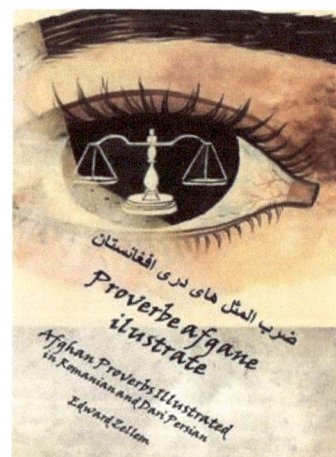
Romanian

More Translations of *Afghan Proverbs Illustrated*

Dutch

Finnish

Italian

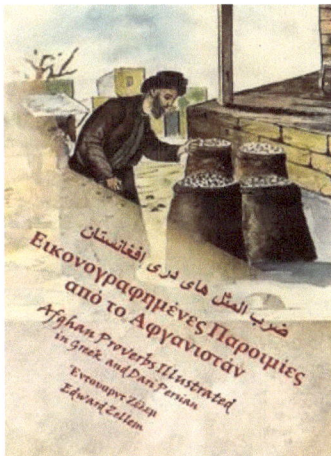

Greek

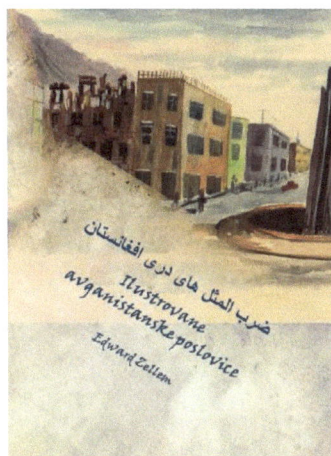

Serbian

Korean

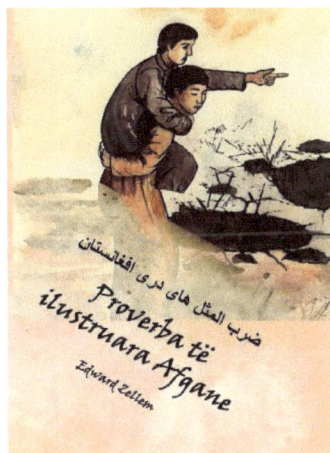

Albanian

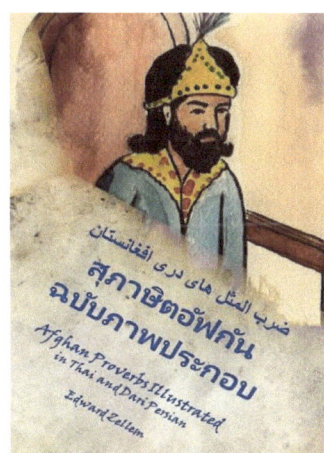

Thai

About the Irish Proverb Scholar And her Associate

Fionnuala Carson Williams

Photo 'Beside the sea in Ireland' courtesy of Lídia Soares

Gordon McCoy

Fionnuala Carson Williams is a graduate of the Department of Irish Folklore, University College Dublin. Although retired she continues to carry out research into proverbs and to publish and speak on them. She is fascinated to see how proverbs from very different parts of the world, such as the pairs portrayed in this series of books, can display common concerns and the glorious variety in the metaphors and references used to do so. For the past while she has been assisting with teaching women whose first language is not English who are living in Belfast in Ireland.

Gordon McCoy is Irish Language Education Officer at the Turas project of East Belfast Mission and has been promoting Irish in schools and in classes of adults for many years.

About the Author

Edward Zellem is a retired U.S. Navy captain, award-winning author and trained Dari speaker who worked every day for a year and a half with Afghans in Afghanistan, including a year inside Afghanistan's Presidential Palace. He served as a United States Navy officer for 30 years.

While in Afghanistan, Captain Zellem became fascinated with the way Afghans use proverbs in their daily conversations. He began collecting and translating them, and used them every day with Afghans in his professional and personal life.

After art students at a Kabul high school created illustrations, his collection first became *Zarbul Masalha: 151 Afghan Dari Proverbs* and then its full-color companion volume, *Afghan Proverbs Illustrated*. Both books were originally published in English and Dari. With the help of other friends of Afghanistan, the proverbs have been translated into additional major languages. After receiving many requests from Pashto speakers around the world, Zellem published a third book: *Mataluna: 151 Afghan Pashto Proverbs*, also illustrated by Afghan students.

About the AIP-IAP
Associação Internacional de Paremiologia-
International Association of Paremiology

The **AIP-IAP** is a non-profit making, cultural institution based in the city of Tavira, located in the Algarve region of southern Portugal. The Association is dedicated to *paremiology*, the scientific study of proverbs. As the only association of its kind in the world, the missions and purposes of the AIP-IAP include:

• encouraging international co-operation in paremiology and related scientific areas;

• establishing action programs with educational officials, public and private;

• encouraging young researchers who are helping to defend, preserve and promote intangible cultural heritage;

• organizing recurring national and international conferences in paremiology;

• promoting studies in paremiology, the scientific study of proverbs.

The quality and quantity of AIP-IAP activities and the published works of its members are recognized by world-renowned experts in global proverbs such as Paremiologists, Phraseologists, and Folklorists. This dynamism has resulted in support from the Municipality of Tavira; the Foundation for Science and Technology; the National Cultural Centre in Lisbon; the Secretary of State for Culture-Regional Directorate of Culture of the Algarve; and UNESCO, which has honored the AIP-IAP by granting it an Honorary Patronage. More information at http://www.aip-iap.org.

The Artists of
Afghan Proverbs Illustrated

Marefat High School Art Department, Kabul, Afghanistan

(Right to Left - 1st Row): Sher Ali Hussaini, Najibullah, Salim, Ali Yasir, Qodratullah, Reza, Ehsan, and Hadi Rahnaward

(Right to Left - 2nd Row): Hamid Fidel, Zainab Haidari, Tahira Jafari, Tahira Mohammadi, Fatima Rezayi, Amena Noori, and Najiba

فهرست Index